The Adventures of

Ogden Nash

Illustrations by Bridget Starr Taylor

SOURCEBOOKS
Jabberwocky
AN IMPRINT OF SOURCEBOOKS

For the real little girl named Isabel who grew up to be just as
adventuresome and courageous as her namesake in the story.

Linell Nash Smith

Thanks to my mother and father
for all they brought to making me.

Bridget Starr Taylor

Isabel met an enormous bear,
Isabel, Isabel, didn't care;
The bear was hungry, the bear was ravenous,
The bear's big mouth was cruel and cavernous.

The bear said, Isabel, glad to meet you,
How do, Isabel, now I'll eat you!
Isabel, Isabel, didn't worry,
Isabel didn't scream or scurry.
She washed her hands and she straightened her hair up,

Then Isabel quietly ate the bear up.

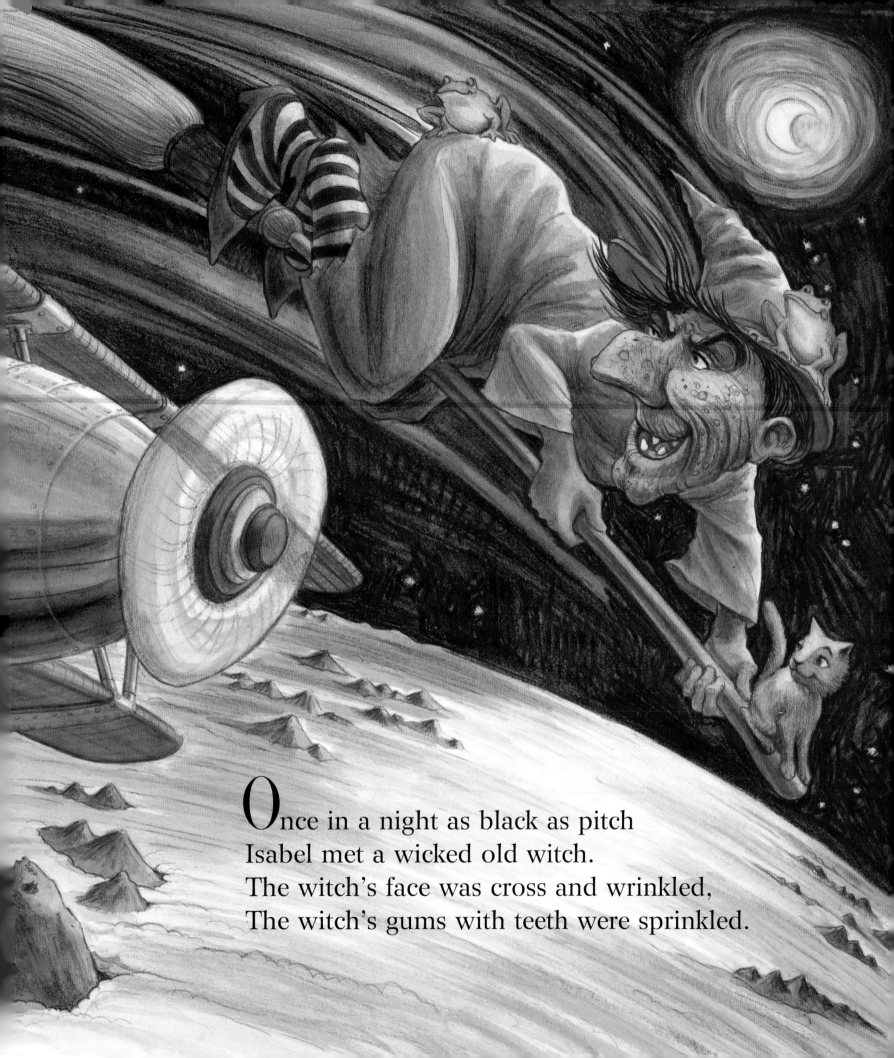

Once in a night as black as pitch
Isabel met a wicked old witch.
The witch's face was cross and wrinkled,
The witch's gums with teeth were sprinkled.

Ho, ho, Isabel! the old witch crowed,
I'll turn you into an ugly toad!
Isabel, Isabel, didn't worry,
Isabel didn't scream or scurry,

She showed no rage
and she showed no rancor,
But she turned the witch into milk
and drank her.

Isabel met a hideous giant,
Isabel continued self reliant.
The giant was hairy, the giant was horrid,
He had one eye in the middle of his forehead.
Good morning, Isabel, the giant said,
I'll grind your bones to make my bread.

Isabel, Isabel, didn't worry,
Isabel didn't scream or scurry.
She nibbled the zwieback that she always fed off,

And when it was gone, she cut the giant's head off.

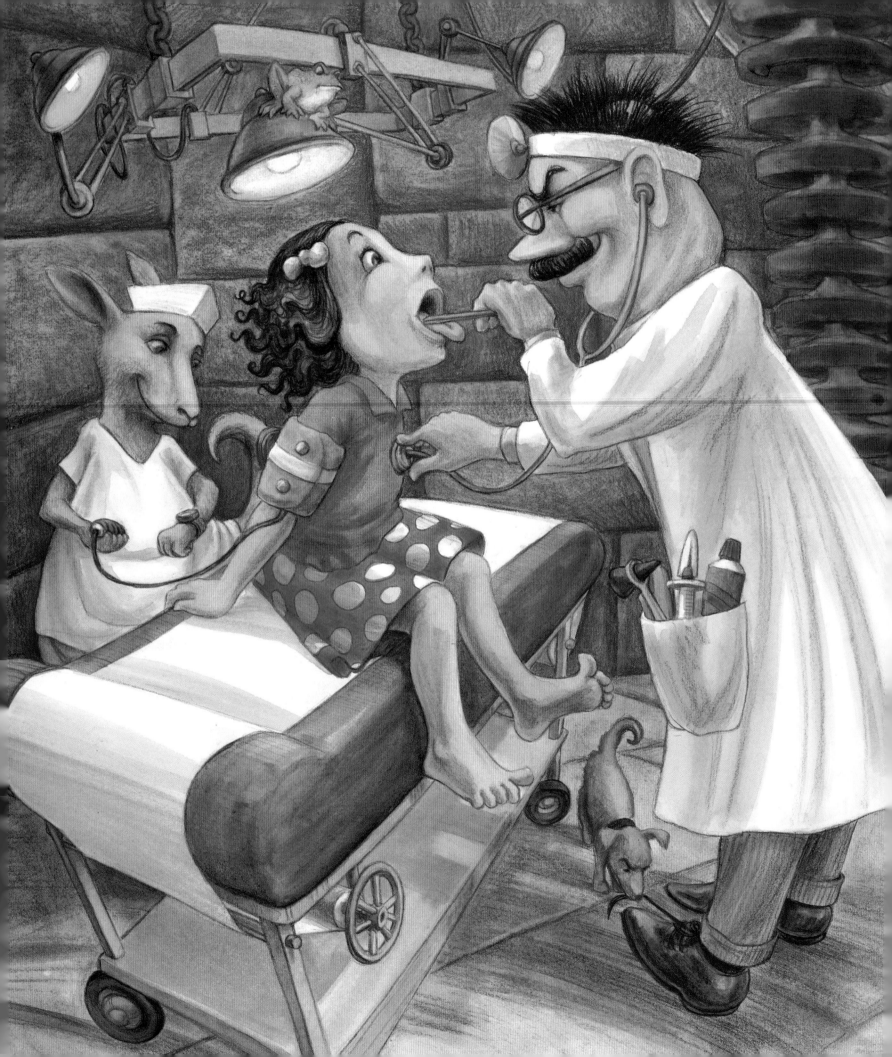

Isabel met a troublesome doctor,
He punched and he poked till he really shocked her.
The doctor's talk was of coughs and chills
And the doctor's satchel bulged with pills.

The doctor said unto Isabel,
Swallow this, it will make you well.
Isabel, Isabel, didn't worry,
Isabel didn't scream or scurry.

She took those pills from the pill concocter,
And Isabel calmly cured the doctor.

This edition of *The Adventures of Isabel* presents the text of Ogden Nash's poem as it was first published in the 1930s. Some thirty years later an extra stanza was added to the classic poem, which has not been included here so that we may present Isabel's adventures as Nash originally wrote them for his daughter, Isabel. Nash's poetry anthologies, as well as his estate, have likewise not included this extra stanza as part of the official version of the poem.

Published by Sourcebooks Jabberwocky, an imprint of Sourcebooks, Inc.

P.O. Box 4410, Naperville, Illinois 60567-4410

(630) 961-3900

Fax: (630) 961-2168

www.sourcebooks.com

Library of Congress Cataloging-in-Publication Data

Nash, Ogden.

Adventures of Isabel / Ogden Nash ; [illustrated by] Bridget Starr Taylor.

p. cm.

1. Children's poetry, American. I. Taylor, Bridget Starr, 1959- ill. II. Title.

PS3527.A637A68 2008

811'.54—dc22

2007043385

Printed and bound in Thailand.

IM 10 9 8 7 6 5 4 3 2 1

OGDEN NASH was born in New York in 1902. He published his first children's book, *The Cricket of Carador*, in 1925. He became well known for his witty verse for grown-ups, including several discussions of men, women, and marriage. He wrote many of his hundreds of poems for his two daughters, Linell and Isabel. They occasionally appeared as characters in his poems, as Isabel does in *The Adventures of Isabel*. Ogden Nash died in Baltimore, Maryland, in 1971.

BRIDGET STARR TAYLOR grew up on a hillside farm in northwestern Connecticut. She received a BA in Illustration from the Rhode Island School of Design. Bridget has lived with her family in a loft in the Meat Packing District in New York City for twenty-five years. She and her husband have two sons, a daughter, and, very recently, twin grandchildren. She and her family spend summers and weekends at the family farm in Connecticut where they have a house of their own. Bridget rides a bike wherever she goes in New York and plays tennis, most often in polka-dotted shorts!

Bridget's mother, Hatsy Robinson, actually attended school in Farmington, Connecticut, with Ogden Nash's daughters Isabel and Linell, and was friends with them both. Hatsy and Linell performed in a small singing group, and sang duets. Hatsy set some of Ogden Nash's poems to music. So Bridget grew up hearing Ogden Nash poems sung by her mother!